Things Y

*A Rhyming Picture Book
For Kids Learning to Read*

*Written and Illustrated

by Steve Hodge*

This is a work of fiction. Names, characters, places and incidents are products of the author's imagination or are used fictitiously. Any resemblance to actual events or locals or person, living or dead, is entirely coincidental.

Copyright © 2014 by Steven Hodge

All rights reserved. Except as permitted under the U.S. Copyright Act of 1976, no part of this publication may be reproduced, distributed, or transmitted in any form or by any means, or stored in a database or retrieval system, without the expressed written consent of the Author.

For information, contact:

stevehodge@mail.com

First Print Edition

If you know how to read

I say, "Good for you!"

And if you haven't yet learned

I say, "That's okay too!"

If you aren't reading yet you'll learn soon enough

Great Stuff

Books
About
Great
Stuff

Even
More
Books
About
Great
Stuff

and then you will read about a lot of great stuff!

Yes, after you've learned
all your A-B-C s
you might read about beetles
and bees that have knees

You might read about lions

and rabbits

and quail

and polar bears

and zebras

and a great big blue whale!

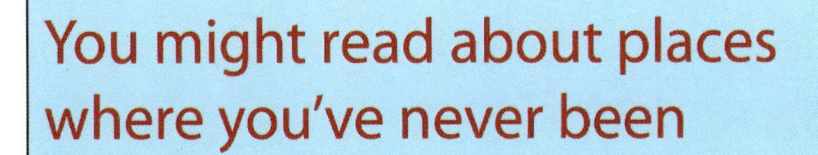

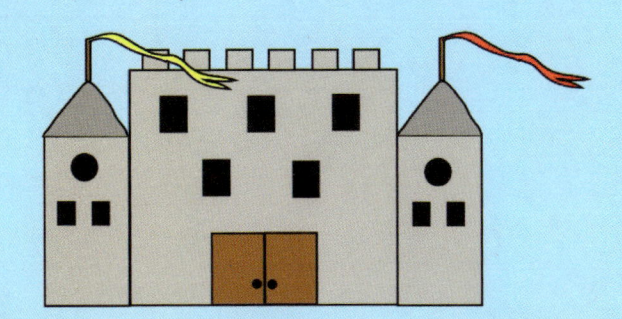

You might read about places where you've never been

like an old Scottish castle

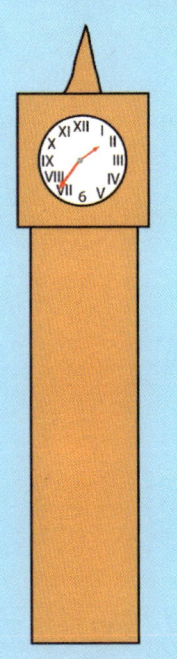

and a clock named Big Ben

You might read about a queen and her silly king

You might read about cupcakes

and here's another thing...

when there's no one to play with
or talk to on the phone

once you learn how to read
you'll find you're never alone!

when nobody's with you
you'll take a book from the shelf

Adventures You Can Have All By Yourself!

and have an adventure
all by yourself!

You might sail on a sailboat

far out on the sea

or fly your own airplane

while you giggle, you see

You might hike through a jungle while searching for gold

or ride in a submarine underwater, so bold!

You might climb a tall mountain and see a house in a tree

or sword fight a pirate
and you might also see

that when you know how to read
you can travel through time

It's easy to do
and it won't cost a dime

You'll go back to see dinosaurs

and Cleopatra's face

then fly into the future
in a rocket through space!

And you'll even find out
with each page that you turn
that it's really exciting
to read things and learn!

You might learn, for instance, how to play a red drum

and you might even learn where hiccups come from!

Then you might learn
how to make your own kite

and if you just keep on reading
it could be, you might...

learn about lizards

and leopards

and lynxes

and people who live far away

and the things that they thinkses

You might learn about windmills

and plants that eat flies

and nice kitty-cats

with different colored eyes

You might learn about planets and galaxies and stars!

and a Viking explorer
whose friends called him Lars

When you're learning to read you won't learn right away

it will take you some time but, hey, that's okay!

Your teacher will help
and your mother and father

and after a while
you won't even bother

to ask for their help
for their help you won't need

and that's when you'll know
that you've learned how to read

Then you'll read funny stories and learn lots of things that you never knew like some dinosaurs had wings!

and about a place they call Egypt
where they have pyramids

and after you're grown *you'll* read to *your* kids!

So be happy you're learning
and though you've just begun

to learn how to read
you'll find reading is *fun*!

THE
END

Other Children's Books by Steve Hodge

Anna and the Storm

Bath Time Can Be Fun!

Bedtime Can Be Fun!

The Can't See 'Em Museum

Count to Ten with Your New Friends

Everybody Farts!

Noel's Christmas Wish

The Seriously Silly A-B-C- Book

The Seriously Silly 1-2-3 Book

Things You Might See

More Things You Might See

Things You Might See #3

Things You Might See #4

The Witch That Was Afraid of Bugs

About the Author

A former educator and graduate of the San Francisco Art Institute, Steve Hodge's rhyming picture book have entertained thousands of children around the world and helped guide countless kids onto the path toward learning to read.

Many of Steve's books became #1 Bestsellers within days of their publication and several were chosen #1 "Hot New Release" the months they were published.

Steve is also a crackerjack ukulele player and is available for inaugurations, coronations, adoubements and other such hoity-toity, nose-in-the-air affairs.

Made in the USA
Lexington, KY
10 July 2017